LAGOON
BOOKS

Puzzle Compilation: Linley Clode and Nick Hoare
Design & Illustration: Linley Clode
Cover Design: James Davies
Editors: Nick Hoare and Simon Melhuish

Published by:
LAGOON BOOKS
PO BOX 311, KT2 5QW, U.K.
CE Keep address for future reference

ISBN 89971 203 8
©1994 LAGOON BOOKS 1994. DR Design Right, Lagoon
Books 1994. Lagoon Books is a trade mark of Lagoon
Trading Company Limited. All rights reserved.

MIND-BENDING

CLASSIC CONUNDRUMS

AND PUZZLES

Also available:

All the Mind-Bending Puzzle books have been carefully compiled to give the reader a refreshingly wide range of challenges, some requiring only a small leap of perception, others deep and detailed thought. All four books share an eye-catching and distinctive visual style that presents each problem in an appealing and intriguing way. Do not, however, be deceived; what is easy on the eye is not necessarily easy on the mind!

A driver notches up 15951 miles on his milometer, and realises that this number is palindromic, reading the same backwards as forwards. He feels pleased to have noticed such a rare occurrence, and is thus doubly suprised when, two hours later, another palindromic number appears.
How fast was he driving during those two hours?

Select any one of the star's eight points. Place a counter on that point, and then slide it along a line to the point at the other end. If you repeat this in the correct way, it should be possible to place and slide seven counters, leaving one point vacant.

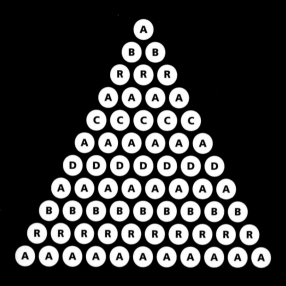

Beginning with the letter A at the top of the triangle and reading down, always passing from a letter to an adjoining letter, how many ways is it possible to read abracadabra?

How can you make a cross from these five pieces?

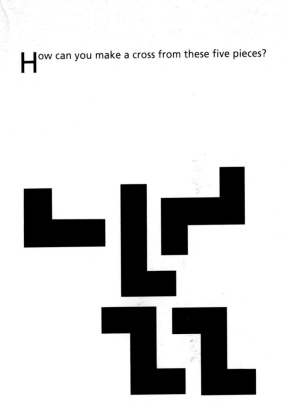

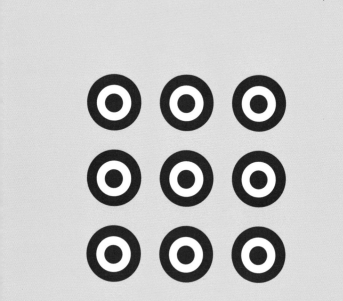

Cross all the dots with four straight lines, without folding the paper or taking your pencil off the surface.

How many of these statements are true?

1 Exactly one of these statements is false

2 Exactly two of these statements are false

3 Exactly three of these statements are false

4 Exactly four of these statements are false

5 Exactly five of these statements are false

6 Exactly six of these statements are false

7 Exactly seven of these statements are false

8 Exactly eight of these statements are false

9 Exactly nine of these statements are false

10 Exactly ten of these statements are false

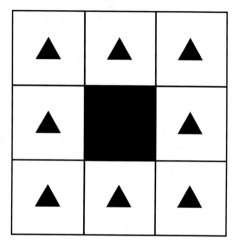

In this building there are eight inmates, one in each cell. How can they be rearranged so there are four inmates along each side?

A traveller found himself in a strange and mysterious country, where the temperature rose sharply during the day, and then fell again at night. He noticed that his watch was 30 seconds fast at nightfall, but at dawn it had lost 20 seconds. On the morning of May 1 the watch showed the right time. By which date was it 5 minutes fast?

Place 6 counters (three of each colour) as shown. The object is to shift the blue counters to spaces occupied by the red counters, and visa versa. You may move counters into empty adjacent squares, and jump over one counter at a time into an empty square. The solution takes 15 moves.

If a partially-filled bottle has a flat base, be it round, square or rectangular, is it possible to calculate the volume of the whole bottle using only a ruler? No liquid can be poured in or out.

A cat dreams that she is encircled by one white mouse and twelve grey ones. She is told she can only eat them all by going round the circle in one direction, eating every thirteenth mouse. The white one must be the last to go. Where does she start?

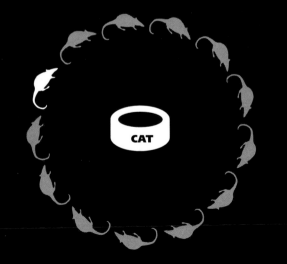

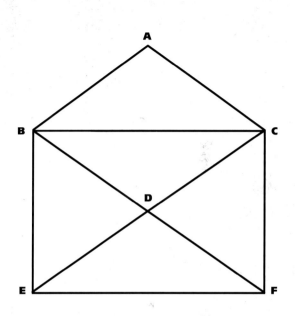

Draw this envelope in one single line, without retracing or crossing any lines, or lifting the pencil.

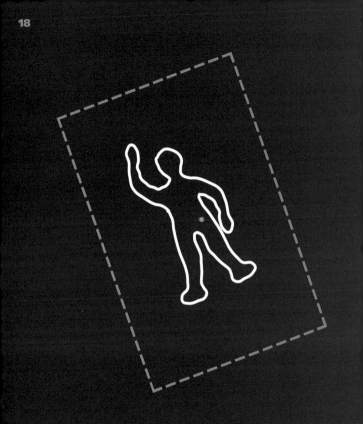

A man lies dead in a field. There is no other living thing in the field with him, but next to him lies an unopened package. How did he die?

Arrange the numbers 1 to 9 in the cells of this square so that the horizontals, verticals and diagonals all add up to the same number.

1 2 3 4 5 6 7 8 9

If you cut along AB and slide the top half one line to the left, one of the lines appears to disappear. Where is it?

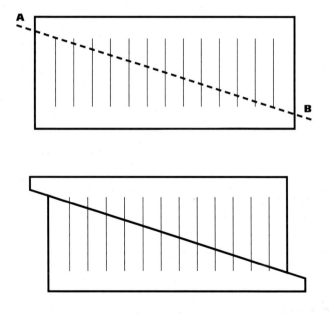

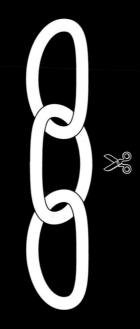

The chain of ribbons shown will only come apart if the middle link is cut. How can three ribbons be linked so that cutting any one of them will free the other two?

A fort with a deep moat is represented with sixteen matches. Adding only two more matches, make a safe 'bridge' to cross the moat.

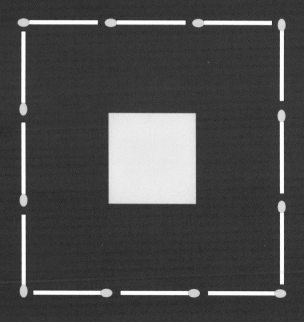

CALMNESS

CANOPY

DEFT

FIRST

SIGHING

STUN

These words share a common feature. What is it?

There are at least 50 million people in the UK, and none of those people have more than 1 million hairs on their head Can we be sure that two people in this country have exactly the same number of hairs on their heads?

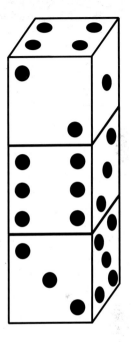

What is the sum of the five hidden faces of these dice?
Why will it always be this sum?

Connect all three utilities to each of the three houses, without any of the pipes or cables crossing.

Form an H with seven coins. Including diagonals, there are five rows of three coins. Add two extra coins to create ten rows of three coins.

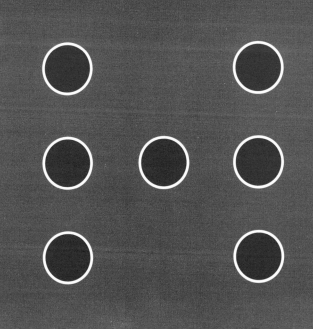

Three men descending a ladder meet up with three men ascending the same ladder. One man can climb over another, but will fall if he tries to climb over more than one man at a time, or walk backwards along the ladder. Is it possible for the trios to exchange places without anyone falling or leaving the ladder?

A sports club arranges a knockout table tennis competition with 37 entrants. How many matches will have to be played to find a winner?

Ηow can you form a cross from the following shapes?

A farmer has nine pigs. Can she put them into four pens so that there is an odd number of pigs in each pen?

tangram. Thousands of shapes can be
se seven. Cut the pieces of the tangra

These four shapes are examples of what can be created. How are they made?

I have two children, who aren't both boys. How probable is it that they are both girls?

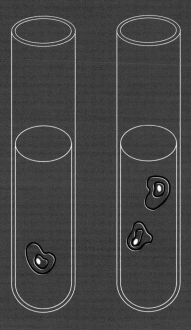

Two amoebas are placed in a test tube. They reproduce by splitting themselves in two, a process that takes five minutes. After four hours they have filled the test tube. How long will it take a single amoeba in an identical quantity of water to do the same?

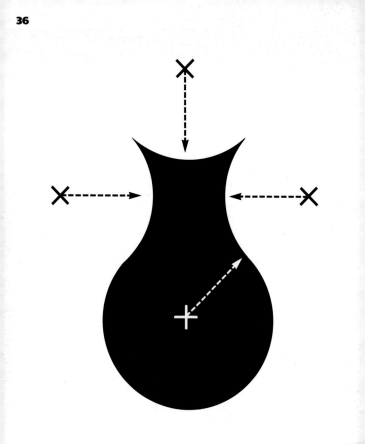

How can you cut this jug into 3 parts with 2 straight cuts and form a square from the parts?

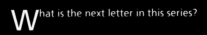

What is the next letter in this series?

How can you place five each of A's, B's, C's, D's and E's so that no letter is repeated horizontally, vertically or diagonally?

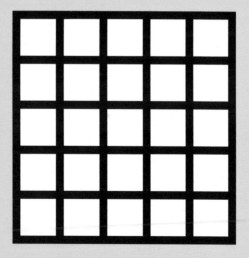

Is this loop likely to be knotted?

A

book

costs

£1 plus

half

its

price.

How

much

does it

cost?

A ferry man has a problem. He has to take a goat, a wolf and a cabbage to the other side of the river. His boat is only big enough to carry two of them at a time. How can he get them safely to the other side without any of them being eaten?

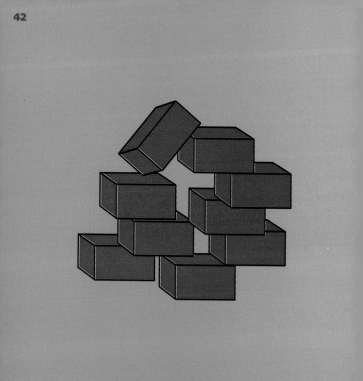

If six bricks are piled on top of each other, but with each overhanging to the left, is it possible for the top brick to completely overhang the bottom brick?

Remove only six matches to make ten. How do you do it?

Remove six cherries from this square to leave an even number in each line and each column. There are many possible solutions.

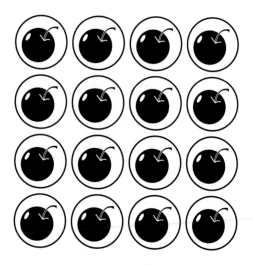

$$
\begin{array}{r}
\text{SEND} \\
+ \text{MORE} \\
\hline
\text{MONEY}
\end{array}
$$

This is a correct addition sum where the numbers have been converted into letters, including zero. What is the original sum?

On a stairway of 100 steps sits a flock of pigeons. One on the first step, two on the second, three on the third, and so on every step up to the hundredth. How many pigeons are there altogether?

These circles are equally spaced. Are there any regions of equal area?

Two thirds of the way into his journey, a cyclist gets a puncture. He is forced to finish the trip on foot, and this walk takes twice as long as the bike ride did. How many times faster does he ride than walk?

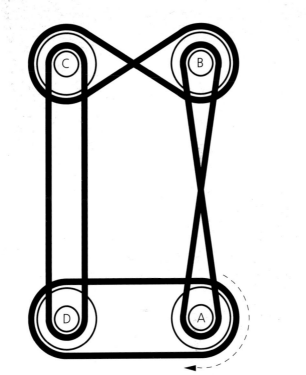

Wheels A, B, C and D are connected with belts as shown. If wheel A rotates clockwise, can all 4 wheels rotate? If so, which way does each wheel rotate? Can the wheels turn if all 4 belts are crossed?

Take a million

Divide it by four

Divide the result by five

Divide the result by two

Divide the new result by twenty

Subtract fifty

Divide by three

Divide that result by eight

Subtract one

Divide the result by seven

Add two

Divide the result by three

Add two

And divide the result by five

Complete the above calculation without the aid of pen, paper, calculator or abacus!

The Chelsea Pensioners (Lewis Carroll)

If 70% have lost an eye, 75% an ear, 80% an arm and 85% a leg, what percentage *at least* must have lost all four?

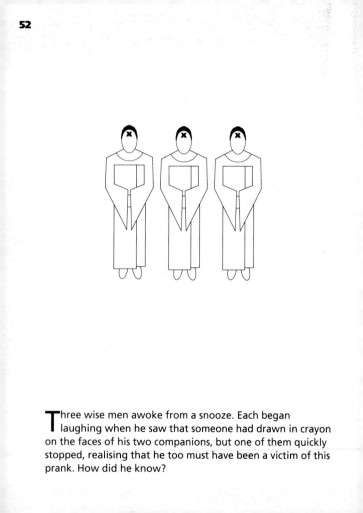

Three wise men awoke from a snooze. Each began laughing when he saw that someone had drawn in crayon on the faces of his two companions, but one of them quickly stopped, realising that he too must have been a victim of this prank. How did he know?

A car departs from A at the same time as a lorry leaves B
The car travels at 65mph while the lorry averages 40mph
Which is farther from A when they pass?

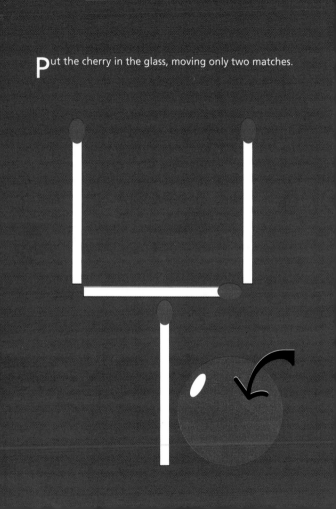

Put the cherry in the glass, moving only two matches.

What are the next two symbols in this series?

A glass of gin and a glass of tonic stand side by side. If you take a measure from the gin and pour it into the tonic, and then take a measure from the tonic and pour it into the gin, does the gin now contain more tonic than the tonic contains gin?

The Serpent's Tail

Drawing only horizontal and vertical lines, two players take it in turns to extend the serpent by connecting adjacent dots to either end of its body. The game continues until one player is forced to connect the snake to itself, thus losing the round.

At the market, a farmer's wife sells half her eggs and half an egg to her sister, half the remainder plus half an egg to her next-door neighbour, half the new remainder plus half an egg to her father-in-law, and half of what was left over plus half an egg to the landlord of the local inn. She is left with one egg, which she takes home and has for her lunch. If she doesn't break any eggs, how many eggs does she start with?

All the following members of a family are present at a family gathering: mother, father, son, daughter, uncle, aunt, brother, sister, cousin, nephew, and niece. Only four people are there. How is this possible?

When the ringmaster died he left all seventeen elephants to the clowns. Bobo got half the elephants, Lobo got a third of them, while Oboe was left with a ninth. Even they knew seventeen can't be divided by two, three or nine, and none of them wished to hurt their four-legged friends, so they asked the lion tamer for assistance. "Borrow one of the lions, pretend it's an elephant, and your problem will be solved." They did this, Bobo taking nine elephants, Lobo six, and Oboe two, with the lion tamer escorting the "temporary elephant" safely back to its cage. So everyone was happy, and the ringmaster's dying wish had been fulfilled. Or had it?

Four skaters spin in circular patterns, each a third of a mile long. They start from the white dots at exactly the same time, and travel at 6, 9, 12 and 15 mph respectively. In twenty minutes, how many times will they have simultaneously returned to the spots where they started?

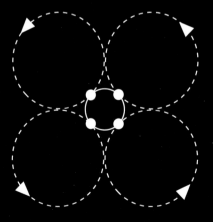

Two sons are

born to the

same woman

at the same

time of the

same day of

the same

year. They

are not,

however,

twins. How is

this possible?

What is the smallest number of these disks that have to be moved to make the triangle point downwards?

At midnight it is raining hard. How probable is it that it will be sunny in 72 hours' time?

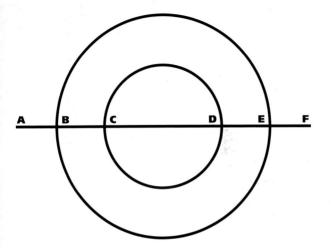

Draw this figure without crossing any line, lifting the pencil off the paper, or going over any line twice.

On a long bus journey with his two grandchildren, a man realises he has left his flask of tea behind. Luckily his granddaughter has brought five cans of lemonade, while his grandson has three. During the journey, they share all of them equally between the three, and afterwards, as a reward for their generosity, he gives them eight 10p coins, telling them to share them in proportion to their contribution of lemonade. They argue long and hard over how to divide the money. How should it be done?

Both the sheep and their owners can move one space horizontally or vertically (not diagonally), with the owners always making the first move. Will they be able to catch the sheep?

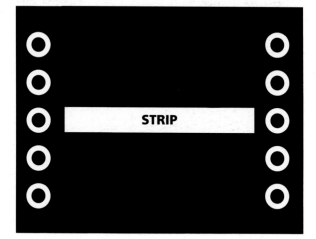

After an evening of intense tangoing, Mr and Mrs Soames, ballroom enthusiasts, wore a strip into their priceless modern rug. To Mrs Soames' relief, her husband, using only straight cuts, divided it into two parts, which when sewn together, formed a square. How did he cut it?

In its
wrapper, a
bar of
chocolate costs
25p. The
chocolate costs
24 pence more
than the
wrapper. How
much does
the wrapper
cost?

A man lies dead in a phone booth. Two windows have been smashed, and there is someone on the other end of the line. Murder is out of the question. How did he die?

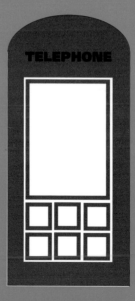

To attend an international summit, the Prime Minister has to catch a 4.00am flight. He has already packed his case, and is getting dressed in the dark to avoid disturbing his wife. His main concern is his socks, which are clean, but not in pairs. He has sixteen black socks and eighteen white socks. How many does he need to be certain of having a matching pair?

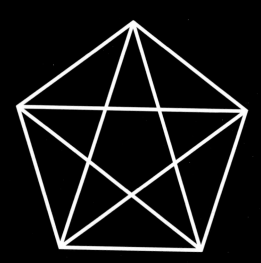

Ⓗow many triangles are there in this figure?

Trace the crayfish, cut out the seventeen pieces, and form a square and a circle from them.

Move just two matches to make seven squares.

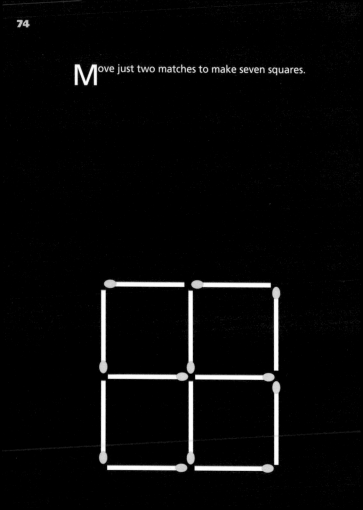

Six glasses, three of them full, are placed in a row. How many moves do you have to make to leave the glasses alternately full and empty?

What gets wetter as it dries?

What mathematic symbol can you put between 2 and 3 to make a number greater than 2, but less than 3?

2 ?< # ÷ ‰ = +] Π ? √ ‡ x ? % ? 3

Use straight lines to join twelve squares in a cross shape, so that there are five squares inside it and eight outside.

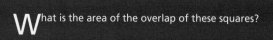

What is the area of the overlap of these squares?

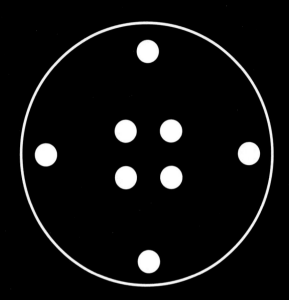

How can this cake be cut into four identical pieces, so that each piece contains two of the smarties and no smartie is cut?

Arrange the numbers 4 to 9 along the sides of this triangle so that each side adds up to 20.

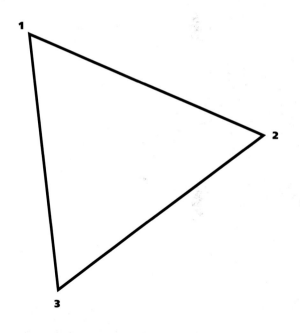

If you write ten letters and place them into envelopes at random, how many letters, on average would end up in the right envelopes?

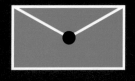

A man in a restaurant complained to the waiter that there was a fly in his cup of coffee. The waiter took the cup away and promised to bring a fresh cup of coffee. He returned a few moments later. The man tasted the coffee and complained that this was his original cup of coffee with the fly removed. He was correct, but how could he tell?

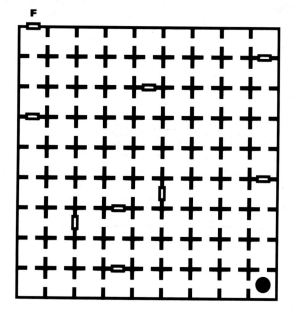

There are 145 doors in this prison. Nine of them are locked. The prisoner (represented by the black dot) must find a route to freedom (F). He can go through locked doors by passing through exactly 8 open doors before each one. He doesn't have to go through every open door, but he must go through every cell and all 9 locked doors. He can't go through the same door twice. How does he escape?

The figure shows a small island, on which is a tree, in the middle of a large and deep lake, which is 300 metres wide. On the shore is another tree (white dot). How might somone who is unable to swim, with only a length of rope rather more than 300 metres long, get from the shore to the island?

If something funny is spelled JOKE, and people can be spelled FOLK, how do we spell the white of an egg?

Mr Berry and Mr Pears each took sixty bananas to market. Berry sold his at two for 50p while Pears' price was 50p for three. After a hard day's selling, the former had £15, while the latter had £10. The following week, to avoid spending all day on their individual stalls, they joined forces, and sold one hundred and twenty at five for a pound (two for 50p plus three for 50p). They took turns at the stall, and sold all their stock. When it had all gone, they totalled their takings and, to their horror, they only had £24. Each suspected the other of stealing the missing pound and they broke off their partnership. Where had the missing pound gone?

solutions

Page 6
The next palindromic number after 15951 is 16061, so he must have travelled 110 miles, giving him an average speed of 55 miles per hour.

Page 7
Move 3 to 6, 4 to 1, 7 to 4, 2 to 7, 8 to 3, 6 to 8 and 6 to 2.

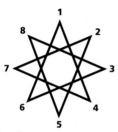

Page 8
The triangle has eleven layers of letters. You have no choice for the first A, two choices for the B, four for the R, and so on, giving you ten stages of choice. This makes the final result 2^{10} or 1024.

Page 9

Page 10

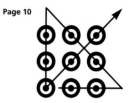

Page 11
All statements contradict each other, therefore one at most can be true, which makes the other nine false. Therefore statement 9 is the answer.

Page 12
To have 4 inmates on each side, place 2 inmates in each corner cell.

Page 13
As the watch is gaining a total of 10 seconds a day, May 31st seems the logical answer, but, as the watch first gains 30 seconds, and then loses 20 overnight, it will be 5 minutes fast for the first time on the evening of the 28th, even though it will only be 4 m 40 secs fast the following morning.

Page 14

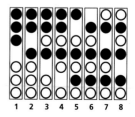

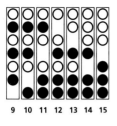

9 10 11 12 13 14 15

4	9	2
3	5	7
8	1	6

Page 15
The area of the bottle's base (y) can be easily calculated with a ruler. When upright, the liquid's volume is y x height of the liquid (l). Turn the bottle upside down and measure the height of the air (a). The total volume of the whole bottle is y(a + l).

Page 16
If the cat starts at the 5th mouse clockwise or anti-clockwise to the white mouse she will eat the white mouse last.

Page 17
Take the following route: E to B, then B to D, then D to C, then C to B, then B to A, then A to C, then C to F, then F to D, then D to E, then finally E to F.

Page 18
The man had jumped from a plane, but his parachute had failed to open. It was the unopened package by his side.

Page 19
This is one of eight possible solutions.

Page 20
No line actually vanishes. Instead, the 13 lines are replaced by 12 lines one twelfth longer than the original ones.

Page 21

Page 22

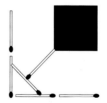

Page 23
Three letters in each word are in their normal alphabetical order e.g. **LMN, NOP, DEF, RST, GHI** and **STU**.

Page 24
Can we be sure that two people in this country have exactly the same number of hairs on their heads?

Yes, we can. If the number of people is greater than the maximum number of hairs on anyone's head, then there are insufficient hair totals for everyone to be different. Some people have to be the same.

Page 25

The top and bottom of the middle die add up to 7 and so do the top and bottom of the bottom die. The bottom of the top die is 3 (7 minus the top of the top die) so the answer is 17.

Page 26

This is impossible unless you take the water pipe for house C, underneath house A as shown.

Page 27

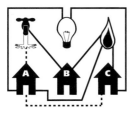

Page 28

Men going down the ladder are labled A,B,C, and the ones going up 1, 2 and 3, in this sequence:

1 A B C ● 1 2 3   **2** A B ● C 1 2 3
3 A B 1 C ● 2 3   **4** A B 1 C 2 ● 3
5 A B 1 ● 2 C 3   **6** A ● 1 B 2 C 3
7 ● A 1 B 2 C 3   **8** 1 A ● B 2 C 3
9 1 A 2 B ● C 3   **10** 1 A 2 B 3 C ●
11 1 A 2 B 3 ● C   **12** 1 A 2 ● 3 B C
13 1 ● 2 A 3 B C   **14** 1 2 ● A 3 B C
15 1 2 3 A ● B C   **16** 1 2 3 ● A B C

Page 29

Knockout competitions run on powers of 2, so a qualification round of 5 matches is required to eliminate 5 players, leaving 32 players who play 16 matches, 16 who play 8 matches, and so on. 5 + 16 + 8 + 4 + 2 + 1 = 36. All knockout competitions need one match fewer than the number of entrants.

Page 30

Page 31

The trick is to put 3 pigs in 3 pens, and then to put the 3 pens inside a larger pen. There are now an odd number in all pens, 3 in three and all 9 contained in the larger one.

Page 34

For two children in general there are four equally likely events: boy-boy, boy-girl, girl-boy, girl-girl. Since boy-boy is ruled out, the probability of two girls is one third.

Page 35

It will take the single amoeba 5 minutes to become two amoebas, so if two need 4 hours, one will need 4 hours 5 minutes.

Page 36

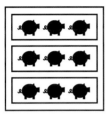

Page 37

The next in this series is **e**. The series is **o**ne, **t**wo, **t**hree, **f**our, **f**ive, **s**ix, **s**even and **e**ight.

Page 38

This is one of many solutions.

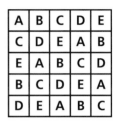

Page 39

There are eight possible sets of crossings at three intersections and only two of these create a knot, so the probability that the loop is knotted is 25%.

Page 40

The price of the book is £2.

Page 41

He should take the goat alone on the first crossing, as there is no danger of the wolf eating the cabbage. He then returns empty and takes the wolf across, but brings the goat back. He then takes the cabbage across, returns empty, and, on his final crossing, takes the goat across for the second time. All three are now on the other side intact.

Page 42

Yes, it is. The top brick can overhang the second by half its length, the second overhangs the third by 1/4, the third the fourth by 1/6, and so on. With six bricks the total would be: 1/2 + 1/4 + 1/6 + 1/8 + 1/10 + 1/12 = 1 9/40

Page 43

Page 44

This is one solution.

Page 45

The sum is 9567 + 1085 = 10652

Page 46

If you add the pigeons on the 1st and 99th steps they total 100, as do those on the 2nd and 98th, and all other pairs. This excludes 50 and 100, so we have 49 pairs equalling 100, plus 150, giving an answer of 5050.

Page 47

As the circumferences of the circles are equally spaced, their areas will be in a square progression; 1, 4, 9, 16, 25, 36, and 49. From this we can see that **25 -16 = 9** and that **25 -1 = 49 -25** (see diagram).

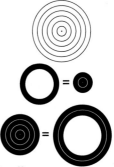

Page 48

The cyclist walks one third of the way, or half as far as he rides, but it takes him twice as long. Therefore he rides four times as fast as he walks.

Page 49

Yes. C and D turn clockwise and B turns counterclockwise. The wheels can also turn if all 4 belts are crossed, but not if 1 or 3 are.

Page 50

The answer is one!

Page 51

30% have got eyes, 25% ears, 20% arms, and 15% legs, so 90% at most have got something, leaving only 10% with nothing.

Page 52

He can simultaneously see both

that the other two are marked, and that they are laughing at him, so a simple deduction tells him that he too is marked.

Page 53

When the car and lorry meet they are the same distance from A regardless of their speeds.

Page 54

Page 55

The symbols are mirror images of numbers, the sequence is 1, 2, 3, 4, 5, 6, and 7, so the next two are...

Page 56

They are both equally contaminated. Provided that the volume of liquid is exactly the same in each glass, then any gin not in the gin glass must be in the tonic, and vice versa.

Page 58

She started with 31 eggs. Half of 31 eggs plus half an egg is 16. She is left with one egg. g is 16. She is left with one egg.

Page 59

There was a brother and sister. The brother's son was there and so was the sister's daughter.

From this, all the relationships can be deduced.

Page 60

The clowns could not possibly comply with the ringmaster's wishes because the fractions one-half, one-third and one-ninth do not total one.

Page 61

In 20 minutes, they travel one third of a mile, 6, 9, 12, and 15 times. The largest number these numbers are all divisible by is 3. They return to their original array 3 times in 20 minutes, after: 6.40 minutes, 13.20 minutes and 20 minutes.

Page 62

They are triplets.

Page 63

Only three disks need to be moved.

Page 64

72 hours later it will be midnight

Page 65

Take the following route: A to B; by upper curve to E; to D; by upper curve to C; straight line to D; by lower curve to C; straight line to B; by lower curve to E; to F.

Page 66

The granddaughter should get

70p, the grandson 10p.

Page 67
They will never be able to catch the sheep nearest them, as they will always be one move ahead of them. They can both, however, catch the other's sheep.

Page 68
He cut the rug as shown in the first diagram, and then put the pieces together as shown in the second diagram.

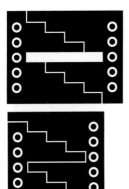

Page 69
The bar of chocolate costs 24.5 pence and the wrapper costs .5p.

Page 70
He was describing to a friend the size of a fish that had got away.

In his enthusiasm, he foolishly demonstrated the size with his hands, breaking the glass and mortally wounding himself in the process.

Page 71
The answer is three socks.

Page 72
There are 35 triangles.

Page 73

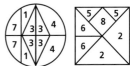

Page 74

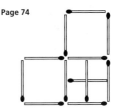

Page 75
Pick up the third glass to the left and pour it into the last glass.

Page 76
A towel.

Page 77
A decimal point.

Page 78

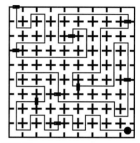

Page 79
The overlap is bounded by two lines meeting at right-angles at the larger square's centre, so it is equal to one quarter of the larger square.

Page 80

Page 81

Page 82
One. It is far more likely that one will end up in its correct envelope than that all ten will be in the wrong envelopes.

Page 83
The man had sweetened the original cup of coffee and therefore after he'd tasted that the replacement was sweet, he knew that he'd been fooled.

Page 84

Page 85
He ties the rope round the tree on the shore, and then carries the rope on a walk around the island. As he passes the halfway mark, the rope wraps around the tree on the island. When he gets back to the original tree, he ties the other end of the rope to it and climbs on the rope to the island.

Page 86

A L B U M E N

Page 87
The two traders made the mistake of averaging the separate rates they charged for the same number of apples. The first week they sold 120 bananas for £125, a rate of 4.8 apples per £1, so the second week saw a reduction in the average price, accounting for the "lost" pound.